MEETING GOD
on the MOUNTAIN
Devotions for Lent

MEETING GOD
on the MOUNTAIN
Devotions for Lent

MARY ANNA VIDAKOVICH

UPPER
ROOM BOOKS

NASHVILLE

Meeting God on the Mountain

Cover Design: Cindy Helms
Interior Design: Charles Sutherland
First Printing: December 1996 (5)

Library of Congress Cataloging-in-Publication Data

Vidakovich, Mary Anna.
    Meeting God on the mountain: devotions for Lent / Mary Anna
Vidakovich.
        p.   c.m.
    ISBN 0-8358-0785-1 (pbk.)
    1. Lent—Meditations. 2. Church year meditations. 3. Devotional
calendars. I. Title.
    BV85.V49 1996
    242'.34—dc20   96-4553
                                                                     CIP

Printed in the United States of America

To John, Joel, Petra, and Hannah
for their constant support,
and to Joyce, because everyone needs help on the journey

CONTENTS

CONTENTS

INTRODUCTION

In the Bible the people of God always seem to be on the move: the Old Testament chronicles the voyage of Noah; the journeys of Abraham, Isaac, and Jacob; the wanderings of Moses and the Israelites; the battles of Saul and David and Solomon; the movement of the people into exile, back from exile, and into exile again. The Gospels detail the journeys of Jesus, which took him from Bethlehem to Egypt and back to Nazareth, from the River Jordan into the wilderness, from Capernaum throughout Galilee and Judea and finally to Jerusalem. Jesus and his disciples were always on the road. Even the Book of Acts and the letters of the apostles have as their background the travels of those preaching and teaching the gospel of Jesus Christ in many parts of the Roman Empire. A good grasp of the geography of the Middle East is helpful when we read the scriptures.

Yet most of us see our own lives as Christians as being settled and unmoving. We have an experience of faith and acknowledge Jesus Christ as Lord and Savior, then settle into a comfortable routine of church attendance, Sunday school, prayer and reading the scripture, and giving of our material resources and our time and talents. But we don't see ourselves going anywhere.

The Christian life is not one of finding a comfortable routine and then living in it for the rest of our lives; the Christian life is a journey that we do not complete until we arrive in heaven. And all along the way, we must search, grow, and change as we seek to know God more deeply, to do God's will more perfectly, to unite with God more completely. As we move along this path our prayer changes, our reading of the scriptures becomes deeper and more personal, our understanding of what it means to live as followers of Jesus Christ in the world remolds our opinions and actions.

The season of Lent is a good time to pry ourselves out of our spiritual easy chairs and take up the journey of the Christian life. By reading and meditating on the scriptures we can see the bad habits into which we have fallen and be reminded of how far our lives are from the life to which Jesus called all who would follow him. But it is not enough just to say, "I'm not where I should be." We must move on to find where and how God is leading us. In what ways and in what areas of our lives is God calling us to deeper communion? deeper understanding? deeper commitment? And if any voice says, "You're fine just the way you are," we can be sure it is not the voice of God!

Resuming our journey begins with repentance. This means repenting of our sins—those actions, thoughts, and attitudes that are not pleasing to God. It also means repenting of our self-satisfaction and contentment with a relationship with God that is not all it could or should be—and as long as we live, our relationship with God will never be all that it could or should be. Repentance leads to confession, which is nothing more or less than admitting we have been wrong, and confession leads to penitence. Penitence is the process of setting things right. We understand that Jesus died that our sins would be forgiven because we could never fully atone for even the least of them. This does not excuse us from doing everything in our power to mend what has been broken by our sin, whether relationships with those around us or relationship with God. Through penitence we show that we are truly sorry and that we know what we should have done in the first place.

Many of the traditional practices of Lent aid our examination of our lives and our repentance, confession, and penitence. Removing the distractions of social events and entertainments gives us time and quiet to focus our attention, to read the scriptures, and to pray. The Lenten fast, which dictates one substantial but simple and meatless meal each day, reminds us how much time and attention we spend on ourselves and our pleasures; the time and money saved by the fast are dedicated to God: for meditation and prayer, for good works and the giving of alms. (Traditionally, children and those in poor health are excused from the fast, although not from the meditation, prayer, and good works that accompany it.) Frequent attendance at public worship—not just on Sundays but throughout the week—focuses our minds and hearts on the worship and praise of God.

Sundays are not counted as part of the forty days of Lent, and penitential practices are not expected on Sundays because each Sunday is a joyful remembrance of the resurrection of Christ. No special reading or meditation is offered for Sundays, just a listing of the scripture lessons for the day. It is hoped that all will make participation in Morning Worship an important part of their preparation for Easter.

Participate in these Lenten disciplines as fully as you are able (not just as fully as is comfortable, for they are not the same thing!).

You are invited on a journey this Lent to search for God—God is not lost, but we often lose sight of God. Throughout the scriptures people had powerful and transforming encounters with God on the mountains and high places of the Middle East. During these forty days, we will revisit some of these mountaintops, listening to what God has to say to us. Set aside at least fifteen minutes, and preferably half an hour, each day to use the *Order for Daily Praise and Prayer* given here. Quiet yourself to enter into the presence of God, and spend time listening as well as speaking and reading. Be open to the changes in your thinking, your actions, and your life to which God may call you.

May God richly bless you in this season of Lent. May your journey with God prepare you to receive the gifts of unconditional grace: the forgiveness of sin through the crucifixion of Jesus on the cross and eternal life through the resurrection of Christ from the dead. Amen.

ORDER FOR DAILY
PRAISE AND PRAYER

Invocation

> God, come to my assistance; Lord, make haste to help me.

Psalm 51:1-17

> Have mercy on me, O God,
>   according to your steadfast love;
> according to your abundant mercy
>   blot out my transgressions.
> Wash me thoroughly from my iniquity,
>   and cleanse me from my sin.
> For I know my transgressions,
>   and my sin is ever before me.
> Against you, you alone, have I sinned,
>   and done what is evil in your sight,
> so that you are justified in your sentence
>   and blameless when you pass judgment.
> Indeed, I was born guilty,
>   a sinner when my mother conceived me.
> You desire truth in the inward being;
>   therefore teach me wisdom in my secret heart.
> Purge me with hyssop, and I shall be clean;
>   wash me, and I shall be whiter than snow.
> Let me hear joy and gladness;
>   let the bones that you have crushed rejoice.
> Hide your face from my sins,
>   and blot out all my iniquities.

Create in me a clean heart, O God,
  and put a new and right spirit within me.
Do not cast me away from your presence,
  and do not take your holy spirit from me.
Restore to me the joy of your salvation,
  and sustain in me a willing spirit.
Then I will teach transgressors your ways,
  and sinners will return to you.
Deliver me from bloodshed, O God, O God of my salvation,
  and my tongue will sing aloud of your deliverance.
O LORD, open my lips,
  and my mouth will declare your praise.
For you have no delight in sacrifice;
  if I were to give a burnt offering, you would not be pleased.
The sacrifice acceptable to God is a broken spirit;
  a broken and contrite heart, O God, you will not despise.

Silent Reflection and Examination of Conscience
    Take time to look back on the twenty-four hours just past. Find the
    times you have experienced God's grace and goodness and the ways
    you have lived the gospel, as well as the times you have fallen short
    and failed to do God's will. Give thanks for God's goodness. Then
    confess your sin and seek forgiveness, rereading the psalm as often
    as necessary to help your prayer. This is not an occasion for self-
    punishment; the goal is to be honest with yourself and with God,
    to receive God's forgiveness, and to make a fresh start for the day
    ahead.

Scripture Reading and Meditation
    Read the scripture lesson for the day slowly and thoughtfully,
    looking for things in the passage you do not remember or have
    not noticed before. If possible, locate the places mentioned on a
    map of the Holy Land. Many Bibles have maps in them. Take time
    to let the scripture speak to you before you go on to the written
    meditation. After you have read the meditation, again take time

to open yourself to what God has to say to you through this passage.

Prayer of Intercession

Lord Jesus, you have sanctified your people with your blood: have mercy on me and forgive my sins.

Loving Redeemer, through your Passion teach me self-denial; strengthen me against evil and adversity. Help me to be ready to join in the celebration of your resurrection.

Grant that all Christians, as your prophets, may make you known in every place by word and deed and may bear witness to you with living faith and hope and love.

Give your strength to all in distress, and help me to lift them up with loving concern.

Teach me to see your Passion in my sufferings and to show others your power to save.

Author of life, remember those who have passed from this world; grant them the glory of your risen life.

The Lord's Prayer

Pray the Lord's Prayer.

Concluding Prayer

Lord, may my observance of Lent help to renew me and prepare me to celebrate the death and resurrection of Christ, who lives and reigns with you and the Holy Spirit, one God, forever and ever. Amen.

The Beginning
of Lent

ASH WEDNESDAY

Genesis 8:1-4, 20-22

Ararat

After the Flood, the ark came to rest on the top of Mount Ararat. It was there, on the mountaintop, that creation was restored as humans and animals came out of the ark to repopulate the earth. And it was there that God made the first covenant with humankind. Many people who know the scriptures well are surprised to find that God had made no covenant with humanity before this moment; there was no promise made by God and guaranteed by God. This makes the covenant with Noah all the more amazing, because in it God made a statement that had to be worked out in practice: "I will never again curse the ground because of humankind, for the inclination of the human heart is evil from youth; nor will I ever again destroy every living creature as I have done" (Gen. 8:21).

A covenant is not a contract that two sides negotiate and both sign; it is a statement of what God will do—and of what humanity will do in response—and it is put in force by God's word alone. In the covenant made with Noah, with all humanity, and with every living thing on the earth, God promised never to destroy the Creation. This is no small thing. Anyone who has worked with clay knows the satisfaction of taking something that has not quite met expectations and of rolling it back into a ball to start over again: The artist has the power to destroy his or her work if it doesn't come out right. This is the power God renounced in the covenant: Never again would God destroy and start over—no matter how bad things became, no matter how far from God's will the Creation wandered.

In our first meeting with God, we are assured that, whatever else may happen, God will not destroy us. We need to grasp and hold this truth. Some try to frighten others into being good by proclaiming that the destructive power of God will surely crush us in the moment of our sin. This is contrary to the very foundation of the scripture. There are punishments and consequences for bad behavior but being utterly destroyed by God is not one of them. God's covenant with us allows us the opportunity to start over, to be better, to amend ourselves and our lives. God gives us the one thing we need to be able to repent, be penitent, and receive forgiveness: life.

This is the basis of our hope. And this is the beginning of the gospel: God will find another way to deal with sin and wickedness; God will find a way to forgive and redeem. The rainbow in the sky is more than a promise that the rain will stop, more than a promise that God will not destroy all life. The rainbow is the symbol of the first steps on the way to the cross and the empty tomb. It defines our relationship with God, and it symbolizes God's determination to save us, whatever the cost.

THURSDAY

Genesis 22:1-14

Jehovah Jireh

Jehovah Jireh, Hebrew for "the Lord will provide," is not one of the familiar landmarks of the Holy Land. In fact, we know nothing about its location except that it is in the land of Moriah. Yet the events that took place there were of great importance for Abraham—and are of great importance for us.

To fully understand what happened at Jehovah Jireh we need to remember the world in which Abraham lived. The people who inhabited the land through which Abraham and his family traveled practiced many different religions and acknowledged hundreds of different gods. Human sacrifice, especially the sacrifice of children, was an accepted practice in some of these religions. When God called upon Abraham to sacrifice Isaac, Abraham's first thought must have been that this God was just like the gods of the people around him. Abraham obeyed because he was bound to this God, but he must have been disappointed that his God was just as bloodthirsty as the rest.

The remarkable thing that happens on Jehovah Jireh is that the Lord God does not allow human sacrifice to be made. The lesson is not that Abraham had enough faith to go through with the sacrifice of his son, although this is usually the focus of our attention. The lesson for Abraham was that this God was different. That continued to be the lesson for the children of Israel as they lived among pagan people for centuries and for the followers of Christ as they were confronted with other religions and other gods. Our God does not ask for the sacrifice of human life, nor does God take away our lives or the lives of those we love to test us or to punish us. Our God refuses to command us to kill in the name of God.

Wealth, success, power, influence, fame, beauty, immortality—the gods of the culture in which we live—all demand the sacrifice of our children, our spouses, our friends, our aged parents, the poor, the helpless, our conscience, and our selves if we are to worship them. When we meet the Lord God on the mountaintop, God will not require us to sacrifice our own lives for our sins, nor will God allow us to kill another living thing to atone for our sins or to prove our faithfulness. Abraham says more than he knows when he tells Isaac, "God himself will provide the lamb for the burnt offering" (Gen. 22:8). Our God is different from all the other gods of the people around us: Our God will make the sacrifice—God not only provides the lamb; God is the Lamb.

In this season when we prepare to see again the sacrifice God is willing to make for our sake, may we free ourselves from all other gods who demand everything and can give nothing. Our God upon the cross gave everything for us. The Lord has provided.

FRIDAY

Genesis 28:10-22

Bethel

Jacob gave up many things when he fled from his father's tents after stealing the birthright and blessing of his older brother, Esau: He gave up family, home, comfort, and wealth. He was also sure that he had given up the God of his father and grandfather and was now completely alone. Jacob's understanding of God—which came in large part from the religions of the people who lived around him and worshiped other gods—was that God stayed with those who worshiped in and around the tents of Isaac and traveled only when Isaac traveled. When Jacob left home, he did not think God could or would go with him.

After a long day on the road, Jacob was too far from any place in which he could find shelter for the night, so he slept on the ground with a stone for a pillow. And God came to him in that isolated spot in the hills. When Jacob woke up he said, "Surely the LORD is in this place—and I did not know it!" (Gen. 28:16). Jacob learned that God can be—and is—found anywhere and everywhere, even out in the wilderness with a runaway boy. Jacob's response was to build a stone pillar as a monument, using his stone pillow, and to anoint it with oil to sanctify it. (This is the Ebenezer mentioned in the hymn "Come, Thou Fount of Every Blessing.") Jacob named the place Bethel, the House of God.

Bethel is one of the most popular names for Protestant churches: We want the place in which we worship to be the House of God. But even if we name every structure we build Bethel, we still will have missed the lesson Jacob learned on the hillside: God is everywhere, and there is no place that is *not* the House of God. The only way to adequately express what Jacob discovered would be to rename the entire universe Bethel—and then we would only have touched on the presence of God in places we can perceive and understand with our limited senses and knowledge.

We look for God on the mountaintop, in the church, at the "holy place." But God is also with us in the valleys and forests and prairies, in every kind of building, and in the most unholy spots we can imagine. This is not always a pleasant and reassuring thought: If God would stay put in the right places, we could go about our lives without worrying about running into God when we are in places or doing things of which we are ashamed. And we would not have to worry about unholy people being able to approach "our" God without our permission. Bethel reminds us that we cannot get away from God—and that we cannot keep God away from those of whom we disapprove.

SATURDAY

Exodus 3:1-12

Horeb

The gods of the people of the ancient world were all local gods: Each one lived in a certain place, dealt with the people of that place, and had no influence or interest in the places and people where other gods were in charge. Horeb was a northeastern peak in a chain of mountains lying between the Gulf of Suez and the Gulf of Aqabah that also included Sinai; in the Bible it is also called Mount Sinai. Horeb had a long history of being visited by a powerful god who caused fire and smoke to come from the mountain. When Moses saw the burning bush on the hillside, it was another sign of this god of the mountain.

As God spoke to Moses, God began laying the groundwork for a relationship between the two of them by naming Moses and his ancestors and affirming again that God was the God of them all. This was not remarkable because Horeb lay in the area that Abraham, Isaac, and Jacob had all visited in their wanderings. But we can imagine Moses' surprise when God began to talk about seeing and hearing what was going on in Egypt where the children of Abraham, Isaac, and Jacob were being held as slaves. Egypt was ruled by Egyptian gods—Moses was familiar with these since he was raised in Pharaoh's household and had probably been taught to worship them as a child. Surely the Egyptian gods now had control over Israel's children! And yet the God of Horeb proposed to send Moses into Egypt to free them. What a remarkable idea: that this God out in the desert was still interested in—could hear and see and care about—people far removed from Horeb! And God's intention was not to bring them to Horeb to live and serve God there but rather to send them on to Canaan—another place entirely, which had its own gods.

Moses had his understanding of the Divine changed that day: no longer was the God of the Hebrews a local god living on Mount Horeb. The God of Abraham and Isaac and Jacob transcended time, remembering promises made more than twenty generations earlier to people long dead, and also transcended place, exercising control not only on Horeb but also in Egypt and in Canaan. We may say, "Why, of course! How could anyone believe differently?" But this was an idea so different that it set the Israelites apart from all other cultures in the area for centuries to come.

We still associate God very closely with "holy places." We make pilgrimages to the Holy Land, to Wesley's England, to the church in which we grew up. Yet we are not lost to God when we are away from these places: God still sees and hears and takes an interest in us, even if we seem to be in a land of foreign gods. And God still asserts that, no matter where we are, God is powerful enough to set us free from whatever bondage holds us and to bring us back into the promise of relationship with God.

The First Week in Lent

Scripture Lessons for Sunday

Deuteronomy 26:1-11
Psalm 91:1-2, 9-16
Romans 10:8b-13
Luke 4:1-13

FIRST WEEK
Monday

Exodus 19:1-9a

Sinai

When God spoke to Moses out of the burning bush, God gave Moses a sign: "I will be with you; and this shall be the sign for you that it is I who sent you: when you have brought the people out of Egypt, you shall worship God on this mountain" (Exod. 3:12). This was definitely not the sort of sign Moses had hoped for: It would come only after all the work was done! And yet, it was a solid guarantee given by God. So it was that three months after they had left Egypt, the Israelites came to the foot of Sinai to worship God—and Moses accepted the sign that it was, indeed, God who had sent him.

We suffer some geographical confusion at this point because we are told that God's promise was made on Horeb and the people actually came to Sinai. Horeb and Sinai are two peaks in the same chain of mountains, and the entire chain was sometimes referred to as Horeb and at other times as Sinai. The exact location of these mountains is not agreed upon by scholars, although it lies between the Gulf of Suez and the Gulf of Aqabah on what we call the Sinai Peninsula.

Up until this point, the Israelites had to trust Moses and the signs God performed through him. When they reached Sinai, they could see the presence of God in a cloud that descended upon the mountaintop. And God gave them their identity in these words spoken to Moses:

"The whole earth is mine, but you shall be for me a priestly kingdom and a holy nation" (Exod. 19:5-6).

Two things are made very clear at this first meeting of God and Israel at Sinai: (1) God is not the God of Israel only, but the God of the whole earth; and (2) the task of Israel is to lead the rest of the world in the worship of God. Keeping both these points in mind did not prove easy.

There is a temptation when we meet God in that transcendent moment of faith we call a mountaintop experience to believe that we have been specially chosen and that God belongs to us more than to anyone else. Indeed, wars, persecutions, and holocausts have occurred because one person or group decided that God was theirs and belonged to no one else.

God reminds us over and over again that God is the God of the whole earth and all the people in it; we cannot exclude anyone for any reason—all are God's. And our role in this world is not to think of ourselves as high and mighty because God has spoken to us. Rather, our role is to be priests by taking the lead in worshiping God at all times and in all places so that the whole world may eventually join in the worship. We are servants of God, workers in God's name, reminders to those around us of the goodness and glory of God. Our work is to lift up God, and never, never to tear down any of God's children.

FIRST WEEK
TUESDAY

Exodus 20:1-20

Sinai

After the first words to Moses at Sinai, God made an appointment with the people, giving them three days to get themselves ready, "because on the third day the LORD will come down upon Mount Sinai in the sight of all the people" (Exod. 19:11). On the third day, with thunder and lightning, thick clouds, fire and smoke and earthquake, God came to rest on Sinai and began to teach the people what was involved in living as a holy people and as God's priests in the world.

The Ten Commandments serve as the basis and summary for all the rest of God's law. The first four points set the people apart from those around them: They are the people who worship God and worship in a certain way. The observance of the Sabbath remains the defining practice of Judaism over four thousand years later. The last six points establish moral and ethical standards of behavior that apply to all people.

When God had finished giving this introduction to the law, the people were terrified. They begged Moses to be their intermediary so that they would not have to see or hear God directly. Moses replied, "Do not be afraid; for God has come only to test you and to put the fear of [God] upon you so that you do not sin" (Exod. 20:20).

How often do we beg to know the will of God, to know what God wants us to do? We are sure that if we could know exactly what God requires and expects, everything would be so easy for us. And yet, when God does speak to us, we react in much the same way as the people at Sinai: We don't want to hear the voice of God. Even attending to the words of God already in our possession in the scriptures proves too much. As simple and straightforward as the commandments are, we mumble and resist and object and make exceptions out of ourselves and our interests until there are no commandments for us anymore. The commandment says, "You shall not murder" (Exod. 20:13). And we say, "Except in war, and self-defense, and capital punishment, and people we don't like, and when there's a good reason." And the commandment has vanished for us because we murder whenever we want.

To meet God on the mountaintop means we must listen to what God has to say to us. Even if it isn't what we want to hear, even if it will require us to change our ideas and opinions and prejudices, even if it frightens us—we must listen. There is no intermediary to soften the words; there is no lawyer to find all the mitigating circumstances that will excuse us. There is only God. This is, indeed, a frightening experience—and it is what we say we want each time we pray, each time we meditate, each time we open the scriptures. God's purpose is only to impress upon us who we are—and who God is.

FIRST WEEK
Wednesday

Exodus 24:9-18

Sinai

Most of us know more about the Book of Exodus from watching the movie *The Ten Commandments* starring Charlton Heston, than from reading the Bible. We can become very confused when the scenes don't match up as we expect them to.

Many things—the movie, most of the Bible stories we were told as children, sermons given on this topic—leave us with the impression that Moses is the only one to go up Sinai, the only one to stand in the presence of God, the only one to hear and see God. Yet, when we read this text, we discover that not only Moses but also Aaron, Nadab, Abihu and seventy of the elders went up Sinai "and they saw the God of Israel" (Exod. 24:10). This is a shocking statement because we have been taught that no one ever actually saw God and that anyone looking on God would be immediately destroyed. Yet these seventy-four people saw God, stayed in the presence of God long enough to eat and drink, and were able afterward to describe the place where God had stood. Before this the people had only Moses' word that God was present on the mountain and that the messages he delivered came from God and not his own imagination; they could accept or reject the law on the basis of their trust in Moses. But when this large group became eyewitnesses, there was no longer any room for questions or doubts.

We were much more comfortable when Moses was the only one

on the mountain. We couldn't expect too much then—and not much could be expected of us since we were getting all this secondhand. Then God called the nameless elders to come up and be witnesses. As Jesus said, "If you know me, you will know my Father also. From now on you do know him and have seen him" (John 14:7). The barriers have been broken down so that we can have firsthand knowledge of God. We can see and hear God for ourselves.

Like the people of Israel, we would rather assign one or two individuals to keep in touch with God and let us know what's going on. But God calls us up the mountainside and appears to us there, and we no longer have the option of ignoring what God has to say to us. This experience of facing God is not for the chosen few, but for all who claim to have faith. It doesn't take, however, the same form for all: We will not all see the floor beneath God's feet appear like sapphire. Indeed, no two of us will have exactly the same experience of God because no two of us are exactly alike. Yet each of us has become responsible for seeking God, for listening to God, and for responding to God for ourselves. There is no one else to do it for us, no one to act as messenger and go-between. We are called up the mountain, where there is lightning and thunder and earthquake, to look on the face of God.

FIRST WEEK
Thursday

Exodus 34:29-35

Sinai

Moses spent a great deal of time with God on Sinai. Others caught glimpses of God, but Moses went up the mountain and stayed there for days on end, wrapped in the cloud that surrounded the glory of the Lord. And the time Moses spent with God changed him.

When Moses first met God, he was a shepherd for his father-in-law, a fugitive from Pharaoh's death sentence. He knew very little about the God of Abraham, Isaac, and Jacob because he had been raised in Pharaoh's palace to worship the gods of Egypt. Moses was shy and stuttered and was in every way the least likely spokesperson for God we can imagine.

Thirty-one chapters of Exodus later we find a calm, confident man worshiping and obeying the Almighty, the Creator of heaven and earth, and delivering God's law to the multitude of people he has led from slavery to freedom. Moses has been changed, and the change is obvious to anyone looking at him. Even if his face didn't shine, we would notice that being in the presence of God has affected this man.

We cannot come into the presence of God without being changed. We will see and understand who God is and who we are. The light of God's righteousness, justice, and truth will shine upon us—and we will no longer be able to deny our sin, our shortcomings, our failures. God will forgive us and make us new—not like we were before but altogether new. When God speaks to us, in any of the many ways God may speak, we will receive direction, guidance, and instruction that will take us in new and unexpected directions. We will be changed.

Before we start scaling mountains in search of God, we need to be sure that we are ready and willing to be changed. If we go only in search of someone—or Someone—to pat us fondly on the head and tell us that we are fine just the way we are, we will be very disappointed in God. We are never fine just the way we are. As long as we live there is room for improvement, there is more for us to learn and understand, there are deeper levels of obedience. If we are content with ourselves, we are deluded. If we do not want to be challenged and changed, we are much better off staying home and leaving God alone.

If we are really ready to seek God, ready to hear and respond to what God has to say, then we know that we have begun our spiritual transformation. Although our understanding and our faith are still imperfect, we are willing to let God work on us, teach us, lead us, guide us. We may not come back with shining faces, but we will be changed.

FIRST WEEK
Friday

Numbers 20:22-29

Hor

Mount Hor (literally "Mount Mountain") on the border of the land of Edom is different from the other mountains and high places we have ascended so far: It was a place of punishment. God had chosen Mount Hor for the death of Aaron. Aaron could not go into the Promised Land with the people of Israel because of his sin. Exactly how Aaron had sinned is a matter of speculation; and while several incidents are suggested, none is clearly identified. In this passage, God cites Aaron's rebellion at the waters of Meribah; a close reading of this incident (Num. 20:1-13) does not reveal the nature of the rebellion, which seems to have been kept between God, Aaron, and Moses. Perhaps this is as it should be: All human beings, from Adam and Eve through Aaron and Moses right up to those now living (with the exception of Jesus Christ), have rebelled against God, and the details are unimportant.

Even while God was meting out punishment to Aaron—and there could be no more severe punishment than to bar him from the Promised Land when the people were almost in sight of its borders—we see evidence of God's continuing love for him. Aaron was warned of what was coming and was able to say his good-byes; he was called up the mountain, into the presence of God; and he departed from the people still in his priestly office, robed and ready to lead the people in worship.

All of us have committed the same sin as Aaron. We have rebelled against God—and not once, but over and over again. With time and prayer and God's grace, the rebellions become smaller and farther apart, but we always seem to cling to the "right" to say, "No!" to God. God loves us and forgives us and gives us the grace and courage to say, "Yes," but God never takes away the freedom that lets us choose our will over God's. God does not turn away from us, and God does not bar us from prayer and worship. We cannot enter the promised land of the kingdom of God while we are in rebellion, so God chooses to stay outside with us until we work through our resistance and willfulness.

Aaron died on Hor and was gathered to his ancestors. God takes us up our own Mount Hor, not to end our lives but to let us see what we are missing and give us the chance to change. In this place of repentance, we are shown the kingdom of God and how far we are from being ready for it. Confronted with our sin, we have the opportunity to strip ourselves of self-interest, self-will, and self-importance. We have the chance to repent and to take up the work of building the kingdom of God in the world by doing the will of God. We come back down the mountain robed for worship and ready to obey when the Lord speaks.

FIRST WEEK
Saturday

Deuteronomy 27:1-8

Ebal

Every nation has a monument that summarizes its history and makes a statement about the way its people see and understand themselves. Usually the monument commemorates a victory in war or a great leader. We have only to see pictures of Washington, D.C., to discover what we understand to be important about the United States: The Capitol building and not the White House has the prominent position because our government is representative and does not rest in just one person. Our heroes are Washington, Jefferson, and Lincoln—men of courage, intelligence, compassion, and insight. When we are at our best, we don't swagger in our victories; instead, we honor our dead for their sacrifices.

Before the people of Israel crossed over the Jordan into the Promised Land, God described the monument they were to build: A pillar on Mount Ebal with all the words of the law written on it and an altar beside it to worship God. It would be a silent reminder of what was important and what defined them as a nation. They were not to commemorate their victories in battle—and there would be many of these in the coming years before the entire land was won and settled under King David. They were not to raise monuments to their own perseverance in the wilderness or to the greatness of their leaders. This nation was to be a nation living under the law of God, a people living to worship God. The pillar and the altar would be symbols to keep them from forgetting who they were.

Mount Ebal, eighteen miles west of the Jordan and thirty-five miles south of Nazareth, could be seen for some distance. Just seeing the mountain on the horizon would be a reminder of the law of God that was written there. No one would have to go up and actually read the pillar; knowing the pillar was there would be reminder enough. After the conquest of this area, Joshua built the monument as God had commanded through Moses, and he read the entire law again to all the people assembled at Ebal (Josh. 8:30-35).

Having a landmark to remind us of the presence and commandments of God is good and necessary because we have such poor memories. Church spires towering above surrounding buildings and large crosses placed on hilltops, serve us as reminders. The great cathedrals were not built to impress people but to witness to the wonder and greatness of God.

Where is Mount Ebal for us? What stands to remind us of God's law and the worship of God to which we are called? What landmark jogs our memories so that we feel compelled to examine our actions and offer our prayers? We must find the landmark we will see daily— the one that will remind us of all the words of God and that will call us back over and over again to seek God and God's will in this place.

The Second
Week in Lent

Scripture Lessons for Sunday

Genesis 15:1-12, 17-18
Psalm 27
Philippians 3:17–4:1
Luke 13:31-35

SECOND WEEK
Monday

Deuteronomy 34:1-12

Nebo

When the children of Israel finally reached the brink of Jordan and were ready, after forty years, to enter the Promised Land, God took Moses to a peak on Mount Nebo, called Pisgah, and showed him all of the land that had been promised to Abraham, Isaac, and Jacob. It is good to read this passage with a map in hand and note the distances to which Moses could see: one hundred miles northwest to Dan, seventy miles west to the Mediterranean (or Western) Sea, another one hundred miles southwest to the Negeb. God granted Moses the privilege of being the first of those who left Egypt to see what would become Israel, and God allowed him to see every corner of it. The promise made to Abraham was delivered to Moses. And then Moses died.

There is something heart wrenching about this man, who has done so much and endured so much, dying within sight of his goal. "Couldn't you at least have let him get his feet wet in the river?" we want to ask God. "Couldn't you have rewarded him with a few steps on the Promised Land?" Even though Moses had sinned and rebelled, wasn't he worthy of forgiveness?

Yet we don't find any record that Moses complained. He was content to have his life and his work end at this point. And God did not seem harsh or punishing. God and Moses were comfortable in each other's company on Nebo, as they had been on Sinai so many years before. When Moses died "at the LORD's command" (Deut. 34:5), God buried him in a place where he would not be disturbed. Moses probably found it very agreeable to die as he had lived: in the presence and the service of the Lord.

Pisgah on Mount Nebo reminds us that we are not immortal. The time will come for each of us to lay down our work, whether we have finished or not. While we resist even thinking about our own death, it is one of the major themes of Lent: The service of Ash Wednesday reminds us, "You are dust, and to dust you shall return. Repent, and believe the gospel." Our lives are not limitless; we do not have forever to repent, to amend our lives, to seek and to do God's will. The time to start is now. And if we are not done when we reach Pisgah, that is as it should be. We will never finish doing God's will on this earth. The best we can hope for is that we will spend every moment of our lives in the company of the Lord, that the title "the servant of the Lord" will be added to our names, and that we will die with our God at our side.

SECOND WEEK
Tuesday

1 Kings 3:3-14

Gibeon

From the time the Israelites had entered the land under the leadership of Joshua, God had been worshiped on many high places throughout the country, with the people bringing offerings and making sacrifices. Gibeon, which means "a high place," was just north of Jerusalem. Because the tent of meeting constructed by Moses was there (see 2 Chron. 1:3), it was one of the primary places of worship in Israel before the construction of the temple in Jerusalem. It was to Gibeon, then, that a young King Solomon went to sacrifice and to pray. While he was there, God appeared to him in a dream and granted his request for the gift of wisdom in ruling his people.

Solomon could have had anything he wanted from God: wealth, power, fame. But Solomon knew what was most important—that he be a good governor for God's people—and he knew what he needed to do a good job. He asked God for understanding and for the ability to discern between good and evil. It is not an accident that the wealth, power, and fame Solomon did not ask for came to him as well as the result of his wisdom.

When we go to God in prayer, how carefully have we considered what we pray for? Are we concerned with meeting the most pressing need of the moment? keeping up with the neighbors or the advertisers? elevating our own comfort and status? Or are we concerned with receiving what we need in order to do God's will? ensuring the well-being of the children of God around us? being able to discern the path of righteousness in our lives? Solomon on Gibeon can teach us not only what to pray for, but—more importantly—how to discover what to pray for.

Obviously, Solomon was already gifted with wisdom or he would not have been wise enough to ask for wisdom. We need to learn to practice discernment so that we can discover how to pray for the ability to know and do God's will. If these seem circular (and they should) it is because our prayer and God's response are not lines that go from A to B to C; they are circles, with God's response to our prayer carrying us to a deeper and deeper understanding of God's will. The gift we most need from God is to know that we need to know more. Only then do we have the humility to ask for help.

Jesus tells the crowds gathered around him: "Therefore I tell you, do not worry about your life, what you will eat or what you will drink, or about your body, what you will wear. . . . Strive first for the kingdom of God and his righteousness, and all these things will be given to you as well" (Matt. 6:25, 33). As we climb the mountain of prayer, we should take time to consider carefully what we need, what is most necessary, and what is God's will. We do this not because we have to make these things clear to God but because we need to have our priorities straight if we are to hear God's answers.

SECOND WEEK
Wednesday

2 Chronicles 3:1-2; 6:18-21

Moriah

When King David suggested that he build a permanent dwelling place for the ark of God in Jerusalem, God refused, telling David that God had always been content to dwell in tents and would continue to do so; to build a house for God's name would fall to David's son (see 2 Sam. 7:1-17). In the fourth year of his reign, Solomon began to build the temple on Mount Moriah at the place David had designated. This building project, begun roughly one thousand years before the birth of Jesus, was of such importance that it shapes the state of the world today.

Solomon kept things in perspective, reminding himself and everyone else that the universe itself was not large enough to contain God and that no structure built with human hands could ever serve as a place for God to live. What Solomon intended in building the temple was to establish one place for worship, prayer, offerings, and sacrifices for all God's people. It was to be a solid reminder of the presence of God in their midst and a focus for all devotions and celebrations of faith. Before too many years had passed, the temple became the only place where worship could be offered or sacrifice made. When Solomon's Temple was destroyed and the people taken into exile in foreign lands, the faith of Israel was almost lost because no one remembered how to worship without that particular building.

We must be cautious not to confuse the presence of God with the place where we experience the presence of God. There is a long tradition in Christianity of putting up a church, chapel, shrine, or museum over every spot where someone has had a significant experience of faith. Often the building soon becomes more important than the faith. Anyone who has toured the Holy Land has witnessed this. And anyone who has seen the closing of his or her home church—the site of weddings, baptisms, conversions, funerals, and other significant family events—knows about this. We confuse the place with the presence of God.

Mount Moriah is still visited by millions of people of faith every year. But it was not the temple that made Mount Moriah sacred; it was the presence of God there with the people who prayed and worshiped. The temple is gone; the presence of God remains.

God does not need a building to live in, and we do not need a building in order to find God. God is present on Mount Moriah in the midst of the city and on Mount Sinai in the wilderness. God is present in the temple and in the laundromat. God is present when we are in our Sunday best and when we are in our bathrobes. The important thing is to focus our attention on the presence of God and to offer our prayers and our worship to God. We must beware the tendency to focus on a building or place, for God will continue when they are dust.

SECOND WEEK
Thursday

Psalm 48

Zion

Most Christians are surprised to learn that the site of Solomon's Temple was Mount Moriah, not Mount Zion. After all, Zion is the one celebrated in the Psalms and the writings of the prophets as the city of God. We assume it is the site of the temple that is being rejoiced over, longed for, prayed toward—but we are wrong.

When David took Jerusalem from the Jebusites, he selected Zion (the word in Hebrew means "fortress"), the highest hill of Jerusalem on the southwestern edge of the city, on which to build his home. He fortified it as the seat of his government. This walled area came to be known as the city of David (see 2 Sam. 5:6-10). The temple was built on Mount Moriah, which lay about half a mile north of Mount Zion.

Understanding this distinction gives us a new perspective on writings, like Psalm 48, in which Zion plays an important role. Zion is celebrated as "the city of the great King" (Psalm 48:2), which is a reference both to David's reign there and to the reign of God that is centered there. Mount Moriah is a symbol of prayer and worship; Mount Zion is a symbol of the power and rule of God. The psalmist uses David's city to proclaim the greatness of God: Zion is a fortress with towers, walls, and gates; a place with strong defenses that no enemy can conquer easily. And God is like Zion: strong and sure, frightening off every enemy.

Mount Zion has become for us only a symbol used by ancient writers; we know that the fortress there was conquered and demolished, and the remains of it now lie far below the city streets of modern Jerusalem, picked through by archaeologists. However, it is still important for us to climb Zion in our spiritual journey, to find again the truth about God that inspired centuries of devotion to this place.

Zion forms the foundation of the kingdom of God that Jesus will later declare as he preaches the good news. Each place in which the kingdom of God breaks into the world is Zion, the city of the great King—places, for example, in which people truly live the gospel that brings good news to the poor, the oppressed, the captive, and the sick. We can establish Zion right here by committing ourselves to live every moment in the presence of God and under all of the rules of the great King. The walls around Zion protect us from the enemies of the kingdom; the walls also hold us close to the presence of God. Zion is not a place to visit or a place from which we commute to the rest of our lives; Zion is the place in which we must live every moment under God's loving gaze. It is the place where we begin to live in the kingdom of God.

SECOND WEEK
Friday

Psalm 125

Zion

Mountains evoke strong emotions in most people. There is a beauty, a permanence, a majesty that inspires us and pulls our gaze toward the peaks. It is difficult to name an ugly mountain: Even Mount St. Helens immediately after its eruption had the marks of terrifying power that drew us to look at it.

In the scriptures, mountains are always symbolic of what is solid, unchanging, reliable. The sea, on the other hand, is changeable and chaotic. The ability to quiet the sea was a miracle; the ability to move a mountain would be a miracle.

It is no accident, then, that God is associated with the mountains and that in the Hebrew scriptures God is so often found on the mountain. The mountains never changed and could not be moved; the mountains were the largest things on the earth, putting human beings in perspective; the mountains were very much like the God whom the people experienced. The psalmist celebrates this enduring quality of the Lord in Psalm 125 by comparing faith in God to the unchanging nature of Mount Zion.

In modern times as we have come to understand nature, we have lost awareness of its awesomeness. We know that the mountains are not permanent but are merely passing features on an ever-changing earth. From our perspective they may appear eternal; but in geologic time, which counts the years by millions, the mountains are moving and flowing like water. Geologists can tell us how they were formed, what they are made of, and how long it will take for them to weather away to nothing.

We have to be careful that science does not erode the mountains of our spiritual life, for we still need symbols that speak to us of the unmoving permanence of God. Perhaps we can revisit Psalm 125:1 and say, "Those who trust in the Lord are *more* solid *than* Mount Zion; *they* cannot be moved, but abide forever." Our trust in the Lord will never be worn away, no matter what storms or disasters may try to break it down. Though all the features of the earth should change, we can continue to trust in God.

The mountains of faith must be approached not with scientific analysis and other such modern "climbing tools" but with the eyes of faith and the bare hands and feet of those who come to stand on holy ground. It is too easy to be cynical and thereby miss the great spiritual truth waiting for us. "As the mountains surround Jerusalem, so the LORD surrounds his people, from this time on and forevermore" (Psalm 125:2). The protective presence of the Lord around God's people will last longer, stand more firmly, be even less likely to be moved than the mountains around Jerusalem. When we come to the mountains of faith, we need to bring with us the phrase, "How much more!"

SECOND WEEK
Saturday

1 Kings 11:1-8

Mount of Olives

Everyone has his or her faults and failings, the kings of Israel no less than the people of today. Solomon, who asked for and received wisdom with which to govern his people, did not seem to have any left over for governing himself and his personal life. He married women whom God had forbidden him to marry: women from other nations who practiced the worship of other gods and turned Solomon away from the God of Israel. In his old age Solomon—who had built the temple on Mount Moriah that God might be worshiped and the people might have a place to pray—built another temple, this one on the Mount of Olives just east of Jerusalem, for the worship of idols and foreign gods.

We must be very careful when we climb spiritual mountains because it is entirely possible to meet idols and foreign gods in the high places and to confuse these impostors with the Lord God for whom we are searching. Solomon's fall from wisdom and glory may make us shake our heads sadly, but it should also stand to warn us of what is possible if we become distracted.

Solomon turned to the worship of other gods because he loved his wives—all 700 of them!—and wanted them to be happy. The desires of his wives, rather than the law and the presence of God, became the driving force of his life and his actions.

It is a trap into which every one of us can fall very easily because there are so many things competing for our attention. Our own bodies are the most immediate distractions, demanding comfort and pleasure. The discipline of fasting is a method of putting the body's demands in their place and of training ourselves to look beyond immediate gratification in making decisions. The advertising with which we are bombarded every day and at every turn tries to entice us into all sorts of worship: of youth, wealth, luxury, consumption, immortality, power, pleasure. The best way to disarm advertising is to ask yourself what each ad is really trying to sell you with the images and songs and catchy sayings, then to ask yourself if this is what you want to worship. Politicians try to seduce us into the worship of idols (ideas and concepts that take the place of God): military power, financial security, the superiority of "people like us" over "people like them," labels such as "Christian" and "family values" with no substance behind them. We are best armed against these foreign gods by understanding the call of the gospel and the true vision of the kingdom of God proclaimed by Jesus Christ. With these firmly before us, no politician or political party can lead us astray.

Remember that the gods on some mountains are idols ready to lead us away from the Lord God. Be awake and alert. Know the scriptures. Do not be distracted by easy answers. Welcome God.

The Third
Week in Lent

Scripture Lessons for Sunday

Isaiah 55:1-9
Psalm 63:1-8
1 Corinthians 10:1-13
Luke 13:1-9

THIRD WEEK
Monday

1 Kings 12:25-33

Bethel

Jeroboam knew that the way to change the politics and loyalties of the people of Israel was to change their worship. He was also smart enough not to try to change over to the worship of the gods of the Canaanites or Egyptians or Moabites. Although Solomon had been converted to these religions by his wives, the people of Israel recognized them as false and foreign and did not follow the king in worshiping at the new altar on the Mount of Olives. Jeroboam realized that the people would not follow any religion belonging to another nation, so he devised a new religion that was very close to the religion of Israel.

Drawing on old traditions in Israel, he turned to the golden calves made by Aaron at the people's request when they thought Moses would never come back from Sinai. He even used the same words to introduce the golden calves: "These are your gods, O Israel, who brought you up out of the land of Egypt!" (1 Kings 12:28; see Exod. 32:1-6). The places selected for the worship of the idols were Bethel and Dan, situated at the extreme southern and northern boundaries of the kingdom of Israel. The priests at these sites were like the Levites—the priests of the Israelites, from the tribe of Levi—but were taken from other tribes. The festival had the same form as the festivals ordained by God. In every way, the religion devised by Jeroboam was familiar and comfortable for the people, but it was not at all the worship of the God of Israel.

We must be even more careful about Jeroboam's shrine on Bethel than about Solomon's on the Mount of Olives. We recognize the foreign gods when we see them, and we do not stay easily or long in the worship of them if our consciences are tender and our knowledge of God and the scriptures is sound. Much more dangerous is the temptation to wrap our own ideas in the trappings of Christianity, surround them with scripture, and try to sell the result as "true" religion. Such distortions of Christianity abound in our culture.

We have to listen and look very closely to see the deception. We have to ask ourselves questions if we are to find the golden calf on Bethel. Did Jesus teach us to hate and revile and attempt to destroy our political enemies? Did Jesus turn his back on the sick and the suffering? Did Jesus tell the disciples to send the five thousand away hungry? Did Jesus tell the little children not to come back until they grew up? It usually takes only the first question to unmask the golden calf that is trying to pull us away from the worship of our God, from the living of the gospel declared and modeled by Jesus Christ. Anyone who tries to divert us from what is written plainly in the scriptures is Jeroboam trying to get us to climb Bethel.

THIRD WEEK
Tuesday

1 Kings 18:17-40

Carmel

Mount Carmel is an impressive sight, rising from the Plain of Sharon and projecting into the Mediterranean Sea between Samaria and Galilee. Carmel was referred to as "the park" and "the well-wooded place"; this was no barren mountain in the wilderness or the desert but a lush, green height overlooking the sea. Carmel also lay within the territory of Ahab, king of Israel, who had his capital in Samaria and "did evil in the sight of the LORD more than all who were before him" (1 Kings 16:30).

Elijah, the prophet of God, had been a thorn in Ahab's side from the beginning, continually proclaiming the Lord's displeasure with Ahab and announcing the punishments God was going to send on him. Ahab, in return, hunted down Elijah in order to silence him once and for all. When Elijah presented himself to Ahab, he proposed the contest between the prophets of Baal and Asherah—gods worshiped by Ahab and his wife, Jezebel—and the prophet of God, Elijah. The contest would determine in the sight of all the people of Israel whether Baal and Asherah or the Lord God was the more powerful. The contest, held on Mount Carmel for all to see, was spectacular, and it could not have been more decisive.

It is important to note that Elijah did not devise the test; he merely put forward what God had commanded him to do (see verse 36).

When we are put in the position of proving that God is with us or that God exists, there is a grave temptation to devise our own tests for God—the more spectacular the better. God is not a tiger trained to jump through hoops at our command. We will be disappointed continually if we put God to such a test because we will be trying to prove our own glory and honor in front of the people who doubt us.

Elijah did only what God commanded. If we could do all that God commands us with the faith and humility that Elijah showed, God would be doing spectacular things every day. The truth is, we spend a great deal of time bargaining with God and giving reasons for not possibly being able to do what we are asked—and rarely are we asked to do anything like battle all the prophets of Baal and Asherah. All we are asked to do is to turn the other cheek, go the second mile, lend without asking for repayment, forgive our brothers and sisters from our heart. We are asked to do unto others as we would have them do to us, to seek first the kingdom of God and God's righteousness, to be doers of God's word and not hearers only (see the Sermon on the Mount, Matt. 5–7).

As we stand on Carmel, we need to pray for the strength and the faith to do the will of God at all times and in all things—beginning with the way we live our lives each day.

THIRD WEEK
Wednesday

1 Kings 19:8-18

Horeb

Things did not go well for Elijah after he killed the 450 prophets of Baal and the 400 prophets of Asherah. Jezebel did not like the idea of her prophets—for she employed them—being killed by some upstart, and she put a price on Elijah's head. Fearing for his life, Elijah ran as far as Beer-sheba, over one hundred miles to the south, but there decided to give up and die.

God was not ready to give up on Elijah—or on Israel—so an angel came to wake Elijah, gave him food and water, and sent him on a journey to Horeb, the mountain of God. It took Elijah forty days to make a trip of over two hundred miles through the wilderness.

God's appearance to Elijah on Horeb was very much like the appearance of God to the children of Israel when Moses brought them to Horeb: there was wind, an earthquake, and fire (see Exod. 19:16-18). People had always assumed that the presence of God caused the wind, fire, smoke, and earthquakes they saw and heard whenever God was near. Elijah learned that God was not to be found in any of these events: the presence of God was in the utter silence. The voice of God could not have reached Elijah through all the noise of wind, fire, and earthquake; and Elijah could not have made himself heard above them. It was in the silence that God invited Elijah to say why he had come and to hear what God intended to do about it all.

When we climb Horeb—or any of the high places—looking for God, seeking guidance or reassurance or solace, we go looking for mighty and powerful signs. We are not prepared for the silence that greets us when we are in the presence of God. Quite often we decide that it is so quiet God must not be there at all, and we turn around and leave. God is inviting us to enter into the silence, where we can hear and be heard. It is in complete silence, when all distractions have been eliminated, that we can tell God what is troubling us, what we need, why we have come—and know that we have God's undivided attention.

It takes this unbroken silence for us to hear God. If we have the voices of our doubts and fears and personal plans carrying on in our ears, God has no chance to make us understand that God has heard us, cares about us, and is doing something about what is troubling us. God has something to say to us, even if it is only that God is with us and we are not alone.

We need to go to Horeb from time to time—away from the noise, the distractions, and all the voices competing for our attention—so that we can speak to and listen to God. Find your Horeb and go there often. Let the wind, fire, and earthquake pass by; then go listen for God, who is always present in the silence.

THIRD WEEK
Thursday

2 Kings 5:1-17

Samaria

Forty-six years after Solomon's death and the division of his kingdom into Israel and Judah, Omri, king of the ten northern tribes of Israel, built his capital at Samaria, about forty miles north of Jerusalem. The hill called Samaria rose behind the new city. Under Ahab the hill had been the site of the worship of idols, but the prophet Elisha reclaimed it for God, establishing his home there.

When Naaman went up Samaria to see the prophet of God, he was in need of physical healing. Of the many skin diseases lumped together under the name leprosy, some were more serious and some less, but all were incurable by normal means. When an Israelite servant suggested that the prophet in Samaria would be able to help, Naaman immediately sought permission from his king to go. He loaded up the gifts he would offer in payment and set out looking for this prophet. It .was the act of a desperate man: He had to cross enemy lines and go into the territory of those against whom he had lately led an army; he could easily have been captured and imprisoned. To add to his puzzling behavior, Naaman did not worship the God of Israel, yet he was willing to ask for God's help.

The change in Naaman was immediate and impressive: not only was he cured of his disease when he overcame his stubborn pride and did as Elisha instructed, he also devoted himself to the worship of God, a very serious act in a society that identified citizenship with the worship of the nation's gods.

It is amazing that even though we know and believe in God, we seldom take ourselves to Samaria in search of healing. We are willing to try all other approaches to healing when we are ill, but for some reason we feel that we have to choose between conventional medicine and prayer. Why are we reluctant to go to the doctor, take our prescriptions and treatments, and pray? Is it because God does not "come out, and stand and . . . wave his hand over the spot and cure the leprosy" (2 Kings 5:11)? Naaman's servants reminded him—and remind us—that being asked to do something to bring about our own cure, even something easy, does not make the cure less effective.

We can be even more reluctant to bring our emotional and spiritual ills to God if we believe that Christians are not supposed to have these problems or feel this way or find life so difficult. So we limp along, even though we know that there is a God who wants us to be well. If that is so, why doesn't God just cure us; why should we have to go and ask, then participate in the cure? Because we have to admit that we are sick before we can be made well. Because coming to God strengthens our faith just as climbing a physical mountain strengthens our legs. Because it gives us the opportunity to say again, "There is no [other] God in all the earth" (2 Kings 5:15).

THIRD WEEK
Friday

Isaiah 2:1-4

Zion

When Isaiah spoke of Zion, he was not referring to a geographical location at the southwest corner of Jerusalem. The Zion of Isaiah's words and visions was something that was yet to come: the center of the reign of God established on the earth. This was not the nation's capital to be built by the descendants of David but the capital of the kingdom of God.

These words of Isaiah must have been difficult ones for many of the people of Judah, the southern kingdom in which Isaiah lived. It was a small kingdom in the midst of powerful countries commanding vast armies. During the time in which Isaiah prophesied in Judah, the kingdom of Israel to the north was conquered by the Assyrians and its people taken into exile. With such events going on around them, the people of Judah were concerned about their own military strength.

Yet Isaiah did not foresee a city of national greatness and power. Zion was to become the capital city of the whole world, a place to which all nations would come. It was not military power but God's teaching and instruction that would be the foundation of Zion's greatness. Living as they did in a world in which all national power was military power, the people must have found Isaiah's vision difficult to understand. Yet in his vision the path of God would be so attractive that people would come from everywhere to learn it, and they would go out to teach it to others in all places.

And another problem for people who lived and died by the sword was that in this world with Zion as its capital, weapons and wars would no longer exist. What would be left to fight over when everyone abided by the word of God, when every person acknowledged God as the great and only ruler?

It is no easier for us to grasp this concept of one rule, one capital, one leader for the whole world, with the teaching of God as the foundation. We cannot imagine giving up our national loyalties and the weapons with which we defend them (in the new world in which we live our weapons are often economic as well as military). It is amazing that those of us who have heard the word of God and accepted the gospel of Jesus Christ are as unable and unwilling to climb Zion and lay everything at the feet of God as the most unrepentant sinner. Why are we afraid of a world in which God rules? Why do we back away from the prospect of a world without boundaries or nations? Will we be the first to go up this new Zion and learn from God—or will we hang back, holding our fears tightly to us? Who is the ruler of our lives?

It is time for us to examine our baggage and discard everything that keeps us from climbing Zion and worshiping before God.

THIRD WEEK
Saturday

Ezekiel 20:40-44

The Mountain of Israel

This unnamed place, which may be more symbolic than geographic, was to be a second Sinai for Israel. The Israelites now in exile are compared to the children of Israel who were slaves in Egypt, and God promises to bring the exiles home again just as their ancestors were brought to the Promised Land (see Ezek. 20:33-38). When those returning reach the holy mountain, God will accept their worship and their offerings. All of this will be done for one reason: "You shall know that I am the LORD" (Ezek. 20:42). One would expect that the response of the people would be rejoicing and celebration. But God warns them that this will bring them face-to-face with their sins.

We think that being in the presence of God is always a wonderful experience—we would bask in God's glory with happy smiles on our faces. Sometimes, however, we respond by saying with Isaiah, "Woe is me! I am lost, for I am a [person] of unclean lips, and I live among a people of unclean lips" (Isa. 6:5). Often times standing before God reminds us of our evil ways and deeds.

As long as we compare ourselves to other people, we can always find some fault in someone else worse than our own. We can always find self-interest and greed more terrible than ours. Even in the saints we find the frail humanity that lets us rejoice that no one is perfect.

It is only when we stand before God, who is perfect light, perfect goodness, perfect justice, perfect righteousness, perfect perfection—only when we stand in the presence of God can we see ourselves as we truly are. And we look pretty bad. There are no mitigating circumstances, no excuses, nothing to do but to see how pitifully short we have fallen when the call was to seek God's kingdom and God's righteousness (see Matt. 6:33).

This is the beginning of true repentance, confession, and penitence. As long as we say, "I've sinned, but I'm not as bad as the guy on the front page of the paper," we have neither repented nor confessed. We must stand alone before God and ask, Have I kept the commandments? Have I lived the gospel? Have I followed the example of Jesus? Have I been a disciple? Have I taken up the cross? And with God's light shining into every nook and cranny, there is nowhere to hide.

Climb the mountain height of Israel where God is revealed. In that place, begin to enter into honest repentance and confession, not making excuses but trusting in the perfect goodness and mercy of God.

The Fourth Week in Lent

Scripture Lessons for Sunday

Joshua 5:9-12
Psalm 32
2 Corinthians 5:16-21
Luke 15:1-3, 11b-32

FOURTH WEEK
Monday

Jeremiah 8:22; 46:11

Gilead

The old spiritual says, "There is a balm in Gilead to make the wounded whole; there is a balm in Gilead to heal the sin-sick soul." Gilead, the mountainous region east of the Jordan that was originally occupied by the tribes of Reuben, Gad, and Manasseh, was famous for production of a balm made from the resin of the styrax tree. The balm of Gilead was used as a remedy throughout the Middle East and was reputed to heal every disease.

When Jeremiah looked on his people, who were in the process of being overtaken by their enemies, he saw their sin as a sickness going to the core of their being, a sickness for which there was no remedy on earth, not even the balm of Gilead.

To climb Gilead is to take the woundedness and sickness of our souls to God for healing. It is not an easy climb. Almost everyone knows the feeling of being too sick to go to the doctor: the journey takes more energy than the sick person has. The soul injured by sin has difficulty thinking of the journey to God, even though it is the journey to healing.

Rather than scale Gilead we choose to remain broken and diseased—and the disease of sin takes over every aspect of our lives before it is done. It eats away at our spirits, souring our outlook on life so that we begrudge others, their achievements and joys. It steals away prayer by whispering that we are not worthy to approach or speak to God. Or, rather than making us feel less holy, the wound may actually make us—like Jeremiah's Israel—think ourselves more righteous than those around us so that we criticize everyone and everything for not meeting our own exacting standards of holiness. We refuse to be healed because we are sure we don't need to be healed.

The truth is, it is absolutely vital to make the journey of confession and repentance. We need to feel the healing balm of God's forgiveness applied frequently. No one is perfect, and none is without sin. All of us are wounded, and only God can heal us. There is no over-the-counter remedy for this, no help on earth. Jesus died to overcome sin and death, to open for all people the path to healing that Jeremiah could not find on earth. We are in need of this healing not just once but over and over again as we fail and fall.

The "Order for Daily Praise and Prayer" on pages 12–14 includes a time to examine our lives and confess our sins every day; the worship services in our churches also frequently include a time of confession. While the pain caused by sin may urge us to avoid these times, each of us needs to take these opportunities seriously and enter into them wholeheartedly. There is a balm in Gilead to heal the sin-sick soul: the balm of Jesus' sacrifice, the balm of God's forgiveness, the balm that will make us whole.

FOURTH WEEK
Tuesday

Habakkuk 3:1-4

Paran

Paran, the hill country, is on the Sinai Peninsula southwest of what was the kingdom of Israel. Reference to it is meant to remind the reader of the first stage of the journey from Sinai to the Promised Land (Num. 10:12), the place David went to mourn the death of Samuel (1 Sam. 25:1), and the region through which Elijah passed on his flight from Jezebel (1 Kings 19:8). In his commentary on this passage, Charles L. Taylor, Jr. says, "God comes to help his people from this region . . . for here was the cradle of Israel's religion" (*The Interpreter's Bible*, vol. 6, p. 998). Like Plymouth Rock or Ellis Island for citizens of the United States, Mount Paran had powerful symbolic meaning for the people of Israel: It was the place from which God would come to help them in their distress.

We often say with great confidence, "God is everywhere." And it is true, verified by both scripture and our own experience. But if we lose Mount Paran, we have lost a real, tangible symbol of what God has done in the past—a symbol that can give us hope of God's acting again for us in the future. When the prophet Habakkuk saw God coming from Mount Paran, he was not saying that God actually lived on a mountain and moved around the earth like a human being; he was saying that God will do again what God has done before.

This is an important mountain for us to keep in our spiritual landscape. We need the reminder that God has acted in us, through us, and around us in the past. We are prone to remember only bad things; failures, hurts, and setbacks haunt us relentlessly while we overlook successes, healings, and advances as being accidents or of no consequence. A part of the examen of consciousness prescribed by Ignatius of Loyola is to recount all of the ways God has been with us in the day, all of the grace we have received. "Count your many blessings, name them one by one; and it will surprise you what the Lord hath done," says the hymn. Indeed, God has been with us and answered our prayers. God has poured out the grace we needed with a bucket and not with a thimble. Mount Paran stands to remind us.

We also need to be reminded that God will continue to act in the same way in the future. While it is easy to say we believe this, we seldom act as if we do. God will continue to be forgiving, loving, and grace-filled in God's relationship with us. God will continue to sustain, support, and strengthen us. God will always be with us in power and glory as in the prophet's vision. Mount Paran stands to remind us.

Look to the horizon of your spiritual landscape and identify Mount Paran, the symbol of God's faithfulness.

FOURTH WEEK
Wednesday

Matthew 4:8-11

The Mount of Temptation

Not all of the biblical mountains are places on a map; the very high mountain to which the Tempter takes Jesus is not an identifiable place but is understood to be a spot from which one could see the entire world. The Tempter shows Jesus "all the kingdoms of the world and their splendor" (Matt. 4:8)—everything over which the Tempter has power. It must have been a dizzying view. Anyone who has stood at the top of the Empire State Building, the Gateway Arch, or Coit Memorial Tower and looked out on cities and towns and countryside can almost imagine it. It was not the smooth view of the earth from space but a detailed look at all the buildings, monuments, and wonders; all the people and animals; all the gold, jewels, and riches. Jesus could command all that he saw; he could enforce his will on rulers and people, if he would acknowledge that the Tempter had supreme power.

A trip to the mountaintop can give us perspective on ourselves and our lives; it can help us to see the greater truths that are lost in the day-to-day struggle through the rocks and trees and brush of the lowlands. A trip to the mountaintop can also tempt us into believing that we own the wonders we see, that we are in control of ourselves and our destinies. The Tempter may, indeed, show us material wealth and secular power, seeking to buy our allegiance with these things; but these temptations frequently are obvious and perhaps we have no difficulty recognizing or refusing them.

A much more subtle and dangerous temptation is to believe that we possess holiness, righteousness, or perfection. The moment we believe that we can no longer fall into sin we are doomed. Jesus gives us the key phrase: "Worship the Lord your God, and serve only him" (Matt. 4:10). Any advance we make in holiness, righteousness, or perfection is a gift of God's grace. Without God's action to defeat sin and death and to bring us to eternal life, we could do nothing. If we believe that we fully understand the scriptures, that our prayer is perfect, that every opinion and thought we have is identical with the will of God, we have been deceived. We work at studying scripture and nurturing prayer and being conformed to the gospel throughout our lives without ever finishing the task. Each step we take is by the grace of God more than by our own efforts—although without our effort and willingness, we would go nowhere.

The Tempter can show us the kingdom of spiritual perfection in an instant, but the only way to get there is by holding the hand of God and walking in the path God lays before us every step of every day of our lives. When we finally arrive at our destination, we will find the kingdom of God and not the playhouse of our imagination.

FOURTH WEEK
Thursday

Matthew 5:1

The Mount of Beatitudes

There is a place overlooking the Sea of Galilee that tradition says is the mountain from which Jesus taught the crowds; on it is built the Church of the Beatitudes. No one knows exactly where Jesus stood or sat or taught; there are a number of hillsides that could just as easily have been the place. Perhaps it is good that we cannot pin the words of the Sermon on the Mount to one specific location; we do not want them to become the word for only one place or time. But the word of God spoken by the Word of God (see John 1:1) had to come from a mountain, just as the law of God had been spoken on a mountain.

The parallel is one we must recognize: The words of Jesus spoken in the Sermon on the Mount (Matt. 5–7) have all the force, the authority, and the binding requirement of the Ten Commandments given on Sinai. Yet we rarely look at the Sermon on the Mount this way; we tend to see it as some idealized portrait of the way things should be in a perfect world, rather than the bare-bones minimum requirements for Christian living. And yet that is exactly what it is: the minimum requirements.

One of the most-quoted verses of scripture is Romans 6:14: "For sin will have no dominion over you, since you are not under law but under grace." Whenever we face any suggestion that the gospel requires us to live in a certain way—to behave toward our brothers and sisters, our neighbors or our enemies, differently than we do—we quote this verse. Then we sit back satisfied that no one—not even Jesus—can tell us what to do because we aren't under the law. We forget to read on through Romans 6:15: "What then? Should we sin because we are not under law but under grace? By no means!" Just because salvation no longer comes through our own actions, by our keeping the law, does not mean that God no longer has any rules for us. The Sermon on the Mount tells us how we must live, loving and praising God in all that we do, now that we are free from the burden of sin.

The message that comes down from this mountain is no more palatable for us than the message from Sinai was for the Israelites. It requires us to change the way we do things, to rearrange our priorities, to look at the big picture from God's point of view. No more revenge or self-aggrandizement; no more showing off our piety. Now we have to give of ourselves, take care of our enemies, be motivated by the common good rather than by profit. We have to learn to live at odds with society and its norms if we are to live out the message from this mountain.

This trip is not for the fainthearted. But it is a requirement for every Christian person, for we are not followers of Christ until we have heard and begun to live the words spoken on this mountain.

FOURTH WEEK
Friday

Mark 3:13-19

The Hills of Galilee

In Greek, verse 13 says, "He went up into the hills. . . ." The northern end of the Sea of Galilee is surrounded by hills, the "mountains" to which Jesus often went to find solitude. After being with the crowds by the sea (see Mark 3:7-12), Jesus went up into the hills to instruct the Twelve privately. It was a great honor to be called apart by Jesus. Earlier he had called on some of them individually to follow him, but at this point Jesus instructed them to preach, to heal, and to be witnesses to all he said and did. The core of the church was formed in the hills above Galilee.

Being called into the presence of Jesus brought both a blessing and a responsibility for the disciples. Being called into his presence is a mixed blessing for us too, if we take standing in the presence of our Lord and Savior seriously.

"Well of course we take being in the presence of Christ seriously!" But do we, really? How often have we invoked the presence of our Lord at the beginning of a meeting and then gone on to act in a way we should be ashamed to have him witness? How often have we prayed for God to be with us in worship, then spent most of the hour thinking of everything but the fact that we stand before God Almighty, Creator of heaven and earth? We so often and so casually pray for God to be with us, then act as if God is unable to see or hear anything we do.

We are called up into the hills of Galilee, into the presence of Jesus, not just for a friendly visit but because he has something for us to do in the world, something for us to do with our lives. This is not a calling only for the clergy, or for those who work full-time in the church; this is the calling for each and every Christian: to be with Christ, to proclaim the message, and to cast out demons (a phrase that includes all manner of healing—physical, spiritual, and mental). We are not excused because we have secular work; Christ's calling is part of our work in the world. We are not asked if Christ's intentions are all right with us; by answering Jesus' call we have already agreed to obey.

Being witnesses for Christ does not mean standing on street corners preaching to all who pass by. We proclaim the gospel wherever we are through our words and our actions—sometimes without any words at all. Likewise, healing is accomplished in a variety of ways: by prayer, yes, but also as we work to feed and shelter the needy; as we share the burdens of others; as we bring the spirit of God's love, acceptance, and grace to those who think themselves outside God's concern. Christian witness is not a limited activity, assigned to a weekly time slot. Our Lord sends us out to proclaim the gospel and heal the world in every moment of our lives.

FOURTH WEEK
Saturday

Matthew 14:22-23

The Hills of Galilee

All of the Gospels tell us that Jesus went alone into the mountains to pray. He needed the renewal, the perspective, the solace that only time alone with God could provide. When we consider the closeness of Jesus with God, the unity they enjoyed in the Holy Spirit, we might wonder why he needed to pray at all. The answer is probably that this closeness and unity was the result of prayer, of open and honest communication between the Heavenly Father and the Only Begotten Son. Jesus was fully human, and a part of our humanity that he shared was the need to put himself in the presence of God in prayer.

We find many reasons to excuse ourselves from prayer or to make prayer a gesture with no substance behind it. How often, when silent prayer is announced in church (especially if it is a silent prayer of confession), do we spend the time not praying but wondering when it will be over? Very few participate in group prayer when it is offered, and we tend to make our private prayer a perfunctory few minutes a day. This is not because we do not want to pray, but because we rarely know how to start or what to do and say.

We may not pray because we feel close to God or because we feel far away. Both are mistakes. Even Jesus needed prayer, and so do all of us—and all the time! None of us is ever without need when we stand before our Creator. Nor can we ever be so far away, so lost, so alienated that God does not hear our prayer. Those who say God hears only the prayers of Christians—or only the prayers containing the proper form of address or the correct closing formula—know neither the scriptures nor God. We need only to use our own words in order for God to understand.

We may not pray because we have nothing to say. This is, in fact, an excellent time to pray because when we are finally done talking we can settle down and really listen to what God has to say to us. Prayer is, after all, two-way communication in which listening for God's guidance, consolation, and direction is vitally important.

We may not pray because we think God fails to answer. In those moments, we need to recognize the grace God gives us to wait on answers that do not come in the time or in the way we think they should. Prayer is not going to the drive-up window and placing an order; it is putting ourselves in the presence of God and waiting there.

We need to go up the mountain of prayer frequently—not every week, or even every day, but as often as we can remind ourselves of it. There is not one aspect of our lives inappropriate for prayer, nothing too small or trivial to lift up to God, nothing too large for God to handle.

The Fifth Week in Lent

Scripture Lessons for Sunday

Isaiah 43:16-21
Psalm 126
Philippians 3:4b-14
John 12:1-8

FIFTH WEEK
Monday

Matthew 15:29-31

The Hills of Galilee

In this passage, Jesus has left the district of Israel called Galilee on the western side of the Sea and has gone on to the largely Gentile region east of the Sea of Galilee. Before this he had healed many among the Jews (see Matt. 14:34-36); now Jesus did the same among the Gentiles, and they responded by praising the God of Israel. The incident is significant because it shows that Jesus was concerned for all people—not only the Jews—and that he would limit neither teaching nor healing to one group. This unnamed place in the hills above the Sea of Galilee might be called the Mount of Inclusion, where all are treated as equals by the Savior of the world.

This picture of Jesus is an important one for us, because we so easily restrict the concern of God to people who are like us. As a society we feel at ease blaming those in need for their state, and we have begun to punish them for it. Persons with disabilities (physical, mental, and so forth) are out of luck. Only those who can pay their own way have a place in our society. And yet, many times when we see Jesus, it was the sick, the disabled, the poor, the hungry, the homeless, the outcast, the demon-possessed who surrounded him and to whom he was ministering. Those who can take care of themselves are instructed to begin taking care of the poor (see Matt. 5:38-42, for example). Through his actions there, in the hills of Galilee, Jesus makes it very clear to those of us trying to live his gospel nearly two thousand years later that we have to live at odds with society; the values of those around us are not the values he wants us to learn and commands us to practice.

So we offer up a compromise: We'll help those in need as long as they belong to our church or as long as they live in our community or as long as they are Christians. And Jesus on the hillside continues to calmly heal the Gentiles, people considered alien and impure in Jesus' own culture. As long as we impose limits on our willingness to help, we have not understood who Jesus is and what he has come to teach us. For Jesus is color-blind; he does not recognize nationality or race or ethnic distinctions. He cannot hear a difference in language or accent or grammar. Jesus never saw anything in those who came to him but their need, and he responded without question to that need.

To come with Jesus into the hills on the eastern side of Galilee is to learn to knock down walls and tear down barriers. Sitting beside him we learn that all are truly children of God, and that God loves and hears and heals all without distinction. And we can then begin to rejoice because each of us was once one of the sin-sick Gentiles coming poor and broken, only to have Jesus graciously heal us because his love is boundless.

FIFTH WEEK
Tuesday

John 4:16-26

Gerizim

The roots of the division between the Samaritans and the Jews ran deep in the history of Israel. When Solomon's successors split his kingdom, Jerusalem continued as the capital of Judah, and Samaria was established as the capital of Israel. Two hundred years later the Assyrians took some of the inhabitants of Samaria into exile and planted foreigners in the midst of those remaining. Because of the resulting mixture of races, languages, and religions in Samaria, the Jews in Jerusalem and Judah looked down on the Samaritans. They had not kept themselves pure. It is interesting to note, however, that the worship of the God of Israel never stopped in Samaria, although the form of worship was not the same as that in the temple in Jerusalem.

When Jesus met the Samaritan woman at the well on the slopes of Mount Gerizim, she had one burning question for the man she perceived to be a prophet: Where should God be worshiped? If the answer was on a mountain, as God had been worshiped for centuries before and after the building of Jerusalem's temple, the Samaritans were right; if people were to worship only in Jerusalem's temple, then the Jews had a point and the Samaritans really were outcast from their God.

It is a question that still cuts deeply across the lives of people of faith. The question of where and how God should be worshiped is the source of division, schism, and dissension in the church, which is supposed to witness to Christ by its unity. We cannot agree on a hymnal, method of prayer, or time of day to meet; we are like the Jews and Samaritans.

Jesus answers that it does not matter where God is worshiped; it does not matter what form that worship takes; it does not even matter whether we come to worship with understanding (a great relief to any who have honestly struggled with the mysteries of God and faith). What matters is our inner disposition to worship–that we are worshiping with willing spirits and as honestly as we are able. This inner readiness matters infinitely more than the color of the carpet or whether the hymns are played on organ or piano or guitar. Jesus opens the worship of God to all who deeply want to worship; we cannot exclude anyone on any grounds. We cannot even require that they "understand," whatever we might mean by that.

When one is climbing in hills or mountains, there are many routes to the top. Some are easier or more direct than others, but all of them reach the goal eventually. Our worship of God is very much like mountain climbing: There are many ways to worship, many forms and orders, and every one of them is acceptable to God. As long as we come to worship with willing spirits and honest hearts, it doesn't matter whether we are in the temple in Jerusalem or on Gerizim—God is there.

FIFTH WEEK
Wednesday

Matthew 17:1-8

Hermon

The site of the transfiguration of Jesus is not identified by name in the Gospels. Tradition had long maintained that this event took place on Mount Tabor, southwest of the Sea of Galilee. Modern scholars think it more likely the Transfiguration happened on Mount Hermon because it is close by Caesarea Philippi (see Matt. 16:13).

Like Moses ascending Sinai with Aaron, Nadab, and Abihu to meet God and confirm his mission, Jesus ascended Hermon with John, James, and Peter. The transfiguration of Jesus was obvious and easily understood, especially after the disciples saw the resurrected Christ: the earthly was stripped away and the glory of God remained to shine on those gathered around. But what about the disciples? What happened to them on the mountaintop?

Peter, James, and John were overshadowed by the presence of God in the cloud, and they heard the voice of God speak to them. And they were also transfigured. The word *transfiguration* means to be drawn differently, to be transformed and remade. The disciples were transformed: beginning on that day, their understanding of who Jesus was changed radically. It was one thing for Peter to say, "You are the Messiah, the Son of the living God" (Matt. 16:16) and quite another to see that truth presented before him. Witnessing the Transfiguration changed Peter, James, and John so that they were ready to witness the resurrection and recognize the risen Christ. They were not made perfect—after all, they later ran from the garden and Peter denied his Lord three times—but the change had begun.

Every time we go up the mountain to be with Christ we must expect to be changed, transformed, redrawn. It is not some tea party we are attending; we go to stand in the presence of the crucified and resurrected Lord. One of the most serious mistakes we can make in the Christian life is to try to stay just the way we are. It is comfortable and requires no adjustment on our part, but it shuts the door firmly in the face of God and precludes any spiritual growth. If we grow, we will change; if God speaks to us, we will change; if we see and understand the power and the glory of Christ, we will change.

The Apostle Paul uses the same Greek word when he says, "Do not be conformed to this world, but be *transformed* by the renewing of your minds, so that you may discern what is the will of God—what is good and acceptable and perfect" (Rom. 12:2, emphasis added). The Christian life involves being changed from what we were and what we are into what we should be. We practice the spiritual disciplines—prayer, reading scripture, worship, receiveing the sacraments, doing good, living the gospel—so that we will be changed, so that we will be able to understand and live according to God's will for us here and now. We come to the mountain to be redrawn.

FIFTH WEEK
Thursday

Luke 19:29-40

Mount of Olives

The Mount of Olives across the Kidron Valley from the northeastern end of Jerusalem was a key site in the last week of Jesus' life. From this high point, he could look over the wall of the city to see the temple (rebuilt by Herod the Great) and the Fortress of Antonia (also built by Herod) immediately to the north of the temple wall—symbols of religious and military power side-by-side. The image was an important one on Palm Sunday.

Standing on the Mount of Olives, Jesus would be able to see the pilgrims who had come to Jerusalem to celebrate the Passover, filling the roads and streaming in at the gates of the city. Word of his teaching and healing, his preaching and miracles had reached nearly every ear as those who had seen Jesus on his travels gathered and shared reports of what they had witnessed. It was no secret that he had come for the feast.

Before he approached the throngs of people, Jesus chose the symbols he would use to describe himself. In the face of those who expected the Messiah to be a warrior-king who would overthrow the Romans and reestablish David's throne, Jesus picked a donkey to ride—a beast of burden and not a warrior's mount. In a challenge to the religious authorities, he allowed the crowds to praise God for his coming. When the Pharisees insisted on a little discipline, Jesus told them, "If these were silent, the stones would shout out" (Luke 19:40). In the face of temple and fortress, Jesus transcended the particular power that each represented.

It is not easy to stand on the Mount of Olives, to be faced by the secular and temporal authorities of our day. More difficult still is to confront these authorities with the gospel and refuse to back down. Jesus accepted the praise, not of the powerful or fashionable or wealthy, but of the common people and the outcast and outsiders. This is the company in which he entered the holy city through the Golden Gate.

We stand on the Mount of Olives more often than we like. We are called on to go into the places of power, but, like Jesus, we are called to go in the company of the powerless—not to protect our position but to use it on their behalf. It would be much easier to stay on the rural hillsides preaching and healing and feeding the hungry. Yet it is impossible to stay there. Sooner or later, the systems that allow people to be sick and homeless and hungry have to be confronted. We have to be reminded with whom God stands—and has always stood. And Jesus admonishes us when we try to sneak in and out unnoticed: If we continue to be silent when the gospel commands us to speak, the rocks and stones themselves will take up the message.

FIFTH WEEK
Friday

Matthew 24:3; Zechariah 14:4

Mount of Olives

At the end of the age and the coming of the Messiah, the Mount of Olives will be at the center of the action. Zechariah gives a startling account of the great earthquake that will take place when God's feet are planted on the Mount of Olives, splitting the hill in two and leaving a wide valley between the halves. In the scriptures, the mountains and hills have always been symbols of permanence; here Zechariah uses a mountain familiar to all the people of Jerusalem to demonstrate how easily God will change even what they are sure is unchangeable. It is no wonder that, seated on the Mount of Olives and looking back at the temple, the disciples asked Jesus to tell them about the signs of his coming and the end of the age.

While in Jerusalem, the disciples acted like all tourists to the big city, oohing and aahing over the buildings—the palaces and fortifications, the theater and hippodrome, and especially the temple compound—and pointing them out to Jesus. Jesus' response was, "You see all these, do you not? Truly I tell you, not one stone will be left here upon another; all will be thrown down" (Matt. 24:2). It sounded very much as if Jesus knew something about what was coming, and the disciples wanted to know how to recognize it and how to prepare themselves. It takes the next two chapters of Matthew for Jesus to tell them all he wanted them to know. His teaching boils down to this: Don't be tricked into following someone else; stay watchful; do what I have taught you and what you have seen me do.

The thought of the end of the world frightens many of us. Even those of us who say we are ready and we will welcome it are probably frightened inside because we do not know how or when or what will come after. Those who claim to have all the answers do not, and Jesus warns us away from them (see Matt. 24:5, 23-28).

So what is there to cling to when everything else is at an end? We hold onto the knowledge that God will still be God, unchanged and unchanging, as trustworthy and reliable as ever. It is not an accident that as part of the lessons about the end of the age Jesus told the parables of the good and wicked slaves (Matt. 24:45-51), the ten bridesmaids (Matt. 25:1-13), and the reward of those who live the gospel faithfully (Matt. 25:14-46)—they are reminders of the faithfulness of God.

What do we do when the earth shakes, the mountains split in two, and the sun and the moon go dark? We do exactly what we should do every day: live the gospel as Jesus preached it and lived it, trusting not in ourselves nor in the material world but in God, who was at the beginning and will be still after the end.

FIFTH WEEK
Saturday

Matthew 26:36-46

Mount of Olives

Jesus chose to spend the last hours of freedom left to him in Gethsemane, an enclosed garden on the lower slope of the Mount of Olives. After being outdoors through so much of his life, under the sun and moon and stars, perhaps he craved these last hours under the trees, with the breeze blowing against his face. So, as he had many times before, Jesus went up on the hillside to pray.

We have so idealized Jesus in Gethsemane that we fail to see and hear the anguish of one who knew he was facing death—and would rather live. We try to smooth it over by saying this prayer was for someone else's benefit, a lesson for the disciples, but it was not; this was the heartfelt prayer of God's only Son to his Father. Jesus really did ask not to die, not just once but three times. Tomorrow he would stand calm and silent before the Sanhedrin, before Pilate and Herod; he would carry the cross without complaint and be stretched out on it without a word; he would die uttering words of faith and forgiveness. But in private on the night before, he poured out before God all his fear and anguish until "his sweat became like great drops of blood falling down on the ground" (Luke 22:44).

Yet this was not all of his prayer. Jesus kept adding one more line: "Not what I want but what you want" (Matt. 26:39). Despite his own feelings, Jesus was determined to do his Father's will even if it meant death. And this is what we have come to the Mount of Olives to learn: to tell God how we feel and then still submit ourselves to God's will.

There is no glory or power on the Mount of Olives this time; we climb the hill because our backs are to the wall and we have nowhere else to turn. We are here to ask God to help us, to make it better, to save us. We know exactly what we want God to do for us! Yet we have one more prayer to learn, one more line to add to our vocabulary as we speak to God: "Thy will be done." And it is not enough to merely say the words—we have to mean them. The most difficult step in the Christian life is the one we do not want to take but must take anyway because it is God's will. We learn, kneeling next to Jesus, how to take that step.

There was no miraculous rescue for him, and there may be none for us. Our only guarantee is that God goes with us every step of the way, never letting us go, never abandoning us when we are doing God's will to the best of our understanding and ability. We don't know how it will all work out; we only know that Jesus did God's will instead of his own, and God raised him up on Easter. If we do God's will instead of our own, God will be with us and will give to us the gift of eternal life.

Holy Week

The Service of Palms

Luke 19:28-40
Psalm 118:1-2, 19-29

The Passion of Our Lord

Isaiah 50:4-9a
Psalm 31:9-16
Philippians 2:5-11
Luke 22:14–23:56

HOLY WEEK
Monday

Matthew 27:33-37

Golgotha

The hill called Golgotha—meaning skull—traditionally is considered to have been outside the wall of Jerusalem to the west, directly opposite the temple and the Mount of Olives. It was the place at which the Romans carried out executions since the Jews would not allow anyone to be executed within the city walls. On Golgotha, Jesus paid the price for the life he had lived.

This is a shocking statement because it is not the way we are accustomed to thinking about the Crucifixion. After all, Jesus was without sin, blameless in the sight of God and utterly obedient to the very end. How could he deserve any punishment at all?

Yet Jesus was executed as a criminal; the authorities wanted to get rid of him quickly. His crime? He challenged their authority, unmasked their greed and self-interest, and took up the cause of the poor and the oppressed in such a way that they could no longer be ignored. To read the Gospels is to read the list of charges against him. Jesus challenged the status quo, and for that he had to pay the price.

We talk about the "victory of the cross," yet at the moment that Jesus hangs on the cross on the top of this hill the only victory belongs to those in power—sin and death have conspired to defeat the sinless Son of God. There is no victory here, except in retrospect; we see it only when we look back from Easter.

We must be careful not to rush past this moment too quickly on our way to Sunday, nor to change its significance in the light of later events. The cross is central because on it Jesus gave up everything—his dignity, his sweat and tears and blood, his last breath, his life—in obedience to God. They were not wrong who wagged their heads and said, "He saved others; he cannot save himself" (Matt. 27:42). It is true Jesus could not save himself; he could only give himself and trust in God's ability to turn the defeat of the cross into victory.

It is a grave temptation for us always to be the heroes of our own stories, to reinterpret events so that we win every battle. When we climb Golgotha we learn that sometimes we lose; sometimes we are condemned by the world; sometimes all we can do is give every ounce of ourselves and then trust in God. If we are faithful in living the gospel in the world, we too will have to pay the price and suffer the punishment set by the authorities of this world for those who challenge the status quo. Obedience to God comes with a price: We give up status, wealth, power, and fame to become like Jesus. In his life and in his death he held nothing back but gave everything to God.

HOLY WEEK
Tuesday

Matthew 28:16-20

A Mountain in Galilee

As Matthew tells the story of Easter morning, both the angel and the risen Christ directed the disciples to go to Galilee, where Jesus would meet them on a certain mountain. This appearance of Christ after the Resurrection and the message he gave the disciples on the mountain in Galilee were so important to Matthew that the evangelist skipped over the accounts of the Resurrection appearances in Jerusalem. Just as Jesus had begun by teaching on the mountain, so he concluded by teaching on the mountain.

We do not know on which mountain in Galilee this meeting took place, although it was evidently well-known to the disciples. It has been suggested that it was Mount Hermon, Mount Tabor, or the Mount of the Beatitudes; no one knows. It is enough that the area that had seen so much of Jesus' ministry also saw his glory.

And that is what we go up the mountain to see on Easter: the power and glory of God, which has raised Jesus Christ from the dead. An important detail of the Easter story is that Jesus did not rise from the dead by his own power. Rather, Jesus, lying dead and helpless, was raised by the power of God (see Matt. 28:6, for example). God's glory now shone undimmed through Christ, so transforming him that at first those closest to him did not recognize him.

We come to the mountain dead in many ways—dead tired, dead

in sin, dead to feelings, dead to those around us—and find ourselves resurrected. We are not brought back to the old life but are filled with a new and eternal life, which overwhelms us. For the story of the Resurrection is not what happened once to Jesus. It is the story of what happens daily to each of us as we strive to listen to God and follow the teachings of the gospel.

Just as we have not been allowed to stay on any of the other mountains we have come to on our journey of faith, the Mount of the Resurrection is not a place on which we can build a home and live. We are only visiting here, for Jesus has not finished teaching, and we have not finished following. The risen Christ in all the glory of God gives the Great Commission (Matt. 28:18-20)—not just to the disciples there that morning, not just to the church as an institution, not just to those specially called, but to every Christian person who would live out what Jesus has commanded. We are sent to all nations, to every person on the face of the earth (those who live next door and down the street as well as those in slums and huts on other continents) to teach them all that Jesus taught us. The resurrection is proclaimed in our living of the gospel every day, in every place, with every one.

HOLY WEEK
Wednesday

Acts 1:6-12

Mount of Olives

The forty days following the resurrection of Christ on Easter were a period of grace unequaled before or since in the history of the people of God. For forty days, the disciples lived in the presence of the risen Lord, traveling along the roads, walking by the Sea of Galilee, sitting at the table, asking questions, being taught, being confirmed in their faith. But the period of grace during which they were equipped to go on as teachers and leaders ended, and the disciples were led out again to the Mount of Olives. There, standing on the hillside, Jesus gave them one last lesson and then was taken up into heaven by God.

The disciples stood, looking up into the clouds waiting for what would happen next. Finally the angels came to nudge them and direct them back to Jerusalem. Our response to being on the mountaintop with God is much like theirs: We want to stay there and wait for the next word from God, the next moment of utterly clear prayer, the next visitation of the Holy Spirit to our hearts. But we are told over and over again that it is not God's will for us to stay indefinitely receiving spiritual blessing—in fact, the blessings will evaporate if we sit too long concerned with nothing but ourselves. We have to go back to "Jerusalem, . . . all Judea and Samaria, and to the ends of the earth" (Acts 1:8).

We go up the mountain as disciples, those who come to a teacher to receive instruction; we come down from the mountain as apostles, which means teachers. The change in terminology is not an accident: Jesus has taught us what we need to know in order to begin, and now he sends us out to teach others. This doesn't mean we have learned everything—a lifetime is not long enough to learn all that we need to know about living the gospel in the presence of God. It means we are ready to teach others even as we ourselves learn more. It is an awesome responsibility, and anyone who thinks it is easy clearly does not understand the task. For we are sent to Jerusalem and Judea—to our family and friends and neighbors, to people just like we who know our faults and failures; to Samaria—to our enemies, the people who hate us on sight, those so different from us we cannot imagine any common ground; and to the ends of the earth—to places and people we cannot even imagine.

The Day of Ascension—the day on which Jesus ascended into heaven—is a sort of graduation day. Instead of being led by the hand, the apostles became leaders. Instead of asking endless questions and receiving constant correction, they became teachers. We cannot spend our lives on the mountain. We must put our faith into practice, put hands and feet to our prayers, and bring the gospel to life in our lives.

HOLY WEEK
Maundy Thursday

Revelation 14:1-7

The Heavenly Zion

The last mountain in the scriptures is again Mount Zion. But this is no longer the earthly Zion, the site of David's fortress and the focus of the messianic hope of the prophets. Zion has been transformed and now stands in heaven. It is no longer the fortress of a king; it is the throne of the King of kings. Angels and elders, living creatures and hundreds of thousands of the faithful worship on this Zion.

We are taken up on the heavenly Zion to glimpse the activity that will fill up eternal life. We speculate constantly about what we will do when we get to heaven, and each of us has a secret notion: endless spring days for golf or summer days for sailing; an infinite mall for eternal shopping or an unlimited supply of our favorite food. We see heaven as that place in which we can do for all eternity what we enjoy doing in this life.

But look from Zion at what occupies all of those around the throne of the Lamb: the continuous worship and praise of God. Throughout the Book of Revelation the images are the same, images of "every nation and tribe and language and people" (Rev. 14:6) devoting themselves to eternal worship. This view should be especially sobering for those who can hardly endure an hour on Sunday morning and five minutes of prayer a day during the week. Heaven may seem a lot like the other place if that is all there is to do!

We were not born knowing how to play golf or sail or shop or eat chocolate or any of the other things we enjoy doing; neither were we born knowing how to worship and praise God. This is something we must learn how to do and then practice doing. And, it seems, learning to worship and praise God with all our body, mind, soul, and strength is vitally important because we will spend eternity doing it.

Those who insist they are already busy enough, and this business of living the gospel takes up all their spare time, and "isn't an hour on Sunday enough?" do not understand. To devote ourselves to the worship and praise of God is not to spend endless hours in the church building going through unending orders of worship. That is just the tip of the iceberg, the way we come together to express what should be going on in many other ways in our lives. All of life can become worship and praise of God—if we allow God into the rest of our lives, if we see opportunities to live the gospel in the busy details of every day. Our insistence on partitioning our lives makes one hour a week "worship" and the rest something else; it is time to take down the walls that divide our lives into compartments and let the Holy Spirit flow through all of our being and doing. Then we will be ready for Zion.

HOLY WEEK
Good Friday

Luke 23:39-49

Golgotha

It is time to climb the hill with the cross once more. This time, however, we do not come as spectators but as participants. The thieves hanging on their crosses on either side of Jesus are all of us: guilty of the crimes of which we stand convicted and receiving a just punishment. All the high-priced defense attorneys in the world cannot get us off because this is exactly where we deserve to be. Our sin nails us to the cross, and we cannot get down. Yet, we have come to the place of God's grace.

We could understand if Jesus at this point had been beyond words, beyond even recognizing his surroundings. He had been beaten and brutalized; he had lost large amounts of blood from the scourging, which stopped just one lash short of a death sentence; he had been forced through the streets and up the long hill carrying.the large wooden cross. We know he lived only three hours after he was crucified, and he must by this time have been very near death. But Jesus was not done teaching or healing or loving the least of his brothers and sisters. The thief did not ask to be rescued or saved—just that he would not be forgotten. And Jesus gave that man so much more than he could have dreamed of asking: Jesus granted him paradise, not at the end of the world or the resurrection of the just, but that very day.

We are fortunate to have our death sentence commuted to eternal life, our punishment turned to paradise when we ask our crucified Lord to remember us. We, who deserve the cross, are given paradise by him who bore the cross. By his example, Jesus teaches us the mercy and grace and love of God; by his words he heals our brokenness and despair. Even though we have helped to put him where he is, he still responds to us with love.

Golgotha was the place of punishment and death; Jesus turned it into the fountain of forgiveness and life. Here, in this classroom, we learn the true depth of mercy and grace that will not allow us to die the death we have earned. And if the Son of God has shown such mercy to us, what mercy ought we to show to one another?

HOLY WEEK
Holy Saturday

The Mountain of Solitude and Silence

On this last day of Lent we climb the mountain of our solitude. This is the day on which we remember the thirty-six hours Jesus was in the tomb, from Friday evening until Sunday's sunrise. This is the day we are alone. The mountain of Holy Saturday is barren and empty: Jesus is not here; God is not here. For that span of hours when Jesus lay buried, the mountains were all empty.

This mountain stands as a reminder to us of all those times in our lives—and we all have them—when we feel God has abandoned us and we are forsaken by our only Friend. We usually do not understand the reason for these times, called dry or dark periods by the spiritual writers. They appear to come upon us for no reason: We have been going along, observing the spiritual disciplines and living the gospel, when suddenly God seems to be gone. Our prayer seems pointless because we feel no one is listening; our reading gives us no insight; there is none of the comfort or happiness we associate with being with God.

These spiritual droughts can be as brief as a few hours or days, or as long as months and years. They present a real challenge to us because as soon as we lose the good feeling associated with spiritual exercises we are ready to quit. "This isn't doing me any good! Why waste my time?" We must remember at these times that we do not pray, read the Bible, make confession, ask for forgiveness, attend worship, or participate in any of the other spiritual disciplines because they make us feel good. If feeling good is my only goal, I would be better off to go eat a chocolate bar. We reach out through prayer and all the other disciplines because this is the only way for us to be present to God, the only way for us to remain open to what God has to say.

If God seems silent for a time, it does not mean that God is absent. Perhaps it is time for us to take the leap of faith that will move us beyond the need for good feelings. Perhaps we are being moved to listen more carefully. Perhaps we are being taught the need to persevere. Perhaps the reasons are God's own. We may understand later on, or we may never know.

Sitting in the silence and aloneness of this mountain, we can be tempted to think that God's back is turned and that, in the face of the Crucifixion, God has walked away from the world and its evil. Or we can watch in wonder as the silent creation prepares itself for the bursting forth of the glory of God in the morning, when the power of the Resurrection will shatter the spiritual landscape and God will be present with us in a totally new and different way. The silence can be the beginning of something grand and glorious: a new chapter of our life with God.

Easter Sunday

The Resurrection of Our Lord

Scripture Lessons for Sunday

Acts 10:34-43
Psalm 118:1-2, 14-24
1 Corinthians 15:19-26
Luke 24:1-12

About the Author

The Reverend Mary Anna Vidakovich is a United Methodist pastor and is currently serving The United Methodist Church in Dorchester, Illinois, and First United Methodist Church in Staunton, Illinois. She was previously the pastor of United Methodist churches in Clinton, Jersey, Calhoun, and Saline Counties in Illinois. She holds degrees from the University of the Pacific (Bachelor of Arts) in Stockton, California; and Saint Paul School of Theology (Master of Divinity) in Kansas City, Missouri. Also, she attended St. John's College in Santa Fe, New Mexico.

Reverend Vidakovich is the author of *Sing to the Lord: Devotions for Advent*. She enjoys needlework, drawing, and quilting. She has three children: Joel, Petra, and Hannah.

• • •

Sing to the Lord invites us to observe the Advent season, rather than quickly usher it in and miss it altogether. In addition to daily meditations for Advent, the author provides a suggested order for daily praise and prayer and a closing prayer for each meditation.